The
Slim-It-Down
DIET
Smoothies

The
Slim-It-Down
DIET
Smoothies

Over 100
Healthy Smoothie Recipes For Weight Loss
and Overall Good Health:
Weight Loss, Green, Superfood and Low
Calorie Smoothies

DIANE SHARPE

Vineyard Publishing

TABLE OF CONTENTS

DISCLAIMER

The information provided in this book is for educational purposes only. I am not a physician and this is not to be taken as medical advice or a recommendation to stop eating other foods. The information provided in this book is based on my experiences and interpretations of the past and current research available. You should consult your physician to ensure that the recipes in this book are appropriate for your individual circumstances. If you have any health issues or pre-existing conditions, please consult your doctor before implementing any of the information that is presented in this book. Results may vary from individual to individual. This book is for informational purposes only and the author does not accept any responsibilities for any liabilities or damages, real or perceived, resulting from the use of this information.

ACKNOWLEDGEMENT

I wish to express my appreciation to my loving and supportive husband, James, who has encouraged me to publish this book. Special thanks to my knowledgeable and experience dietitian friend Maria for her unwavering support and also to all my family and friends for enjoying and critiquing my recipes through the years.

READ THIS FIRST!

Proven weight loss results and optimal health – that's what you get with the *Slim-It-Down Diet Smoothies.*

My name is Diane Sharpe and I love *Slim-It-Down Diet Smoothies* for lots of reasons. I love the tasty flavors, simple ingredients and natural foods without worrying about the dangers of artificial foods, heavy carbs and loads of hidden sugar. But, even more importantly, I love the life changing results that I've received from drinking these smoothies. That's why I am so excited to share my healthy and life changing "Slim-It-Down Diet Smoothies" with everyone.

I hope that they will be well-received with readers as they have been with my family and friends. By combining these smoothies with a particular regime (which I will explain later), my health has been completely restored. I am committed to sharing my success with everyone and I will be drinking one of these smoothies until I take my last breath.

IS THIS A RIDICULOUS FAD DIET?

No, the *Slim-It-Down Diet Smoothies* are healthy smoothies in support of a healthy lifestyle. These diet smoothies are not just an impractical diet regime that promises unrealistic health results. For instance, unlike some other diets, the *Slim-It-Down Diet* regime does not support the diet notion of: "eating more food to lose weight" or "eating whatever you want". That would be senseless; our bodies were creatively and specially designed for us to eat certain foods to stay healthy. I like to put it this way: Junk in; Junk out!

IS THE SLIM-IT-DOWN DIET SMOOTHIES FOR ME?

Yes. With this wholesome approach and a variety of over 100 specially crafted healthy smoothies, you are sure to find some favorite smoothies to tickle your fancy and improve your health. In this book you'll find a combination of smoothie recipes that are:

- **Healthy for everyone**
- **Low Calorie** (Between 100 - 300 calories)
- **Low Carb**
- **Low Fat**
- **High Protein**
- **Sugar-Free**
- **Dairy-Free**
- **Vegan Friendly**

WHO IS THIS DIET FOR?

- Anyone who wishes to lose weight or just improve their overall vitality or boost their immunity
- Anyone on the FAST DIET, 5:2 DIET or OVERNIGHT DIET Regime
- Wheat-Free Dieters
- Smoothie lovers who really appreciate a wholesome and healthy drink
- Vegetarians who understand the power of vegetables and fruits
- Paleo Dieters

HOW ABOUT MY PROTEIN INTAKE?

Yes, protein is important in your diet. You'll find more than enough smoothies with healthy protein content that will make this diet effective. You'll learn more about the importance of protein intake later in the chapter: EXPECT A HEALTHY SMOOTHIE AND NOTHING LESS.

HERE'S MY STORY...

Prior to 2009, I was terribly obese and I'd spent thousands of dollars on medical bills. Year after year, different doctors had always concluded that I may not lose the amount of weight that I wanted to lose, because "it runs in my family".

Well, I have proved them wrong – and here's the best part, I did it the healthy way. I have successfully retrained my "fat genes" and I've finally been able to lose weight for good and maintain my best health.

MY TURNING POINT...

Yes, I too, was a victim of several fad diets which I had tried out of desperation and I had genuine confidence that they actually worked. I was caught in the "lose weight without dieting" gimmick and many others. The sad reality is that I could hardly ever manage to stick to any one of these diets for as little as two weeks. I would often feel sick, dizzy and worse than I did before. Or even worst, I literally had little or no energy at all and usually regained the weight that I'd initially lost.

As I continued to pile on the pounds, my health continued to worsen. I was faced with a do or die situation, so I decided that I needed to take serious actions if I wanted to get well.

HOW I DID IT...

Fortunately, during my quest for better health, a friend of mine (thanks again Maria) invited me to an enlightening *Wellness Series Seminar* in the Washington area. The experience was amazing! The registered dieticians delivered detailed wellness information in such a way that it was easy to understand. As a result, I left fully motivated and got priceless insight about how I could effectively transform my life on a smoothie diet. Since then, wherever I go, I would gather new information from smoothie fans and registered dieticians worldwide. Through everyday blending, additional extensive research, experience, and feedback from my friend and family circles, I came up with my very own "Slim-It-Down Diet Smoothies". The long and short of it all, is that it took time for me to get it right.

In 2009, I stayed on a one-day per week smoothie diet which I called my "**Smoothie Fasting Day**". I didn't deviate from this diet regime for six (6) months. I was determined to get rid of my health problems for good. During this six month period, my weight and other health problems significantly improved, so I knew the *Slim-It-Down Diet Smoothies* really worked. Consequently, I've managed to lose over 50 pounds in 6 months and to date I've lost a total of 115 pounds. I was also able to TOTALLY overcome high cholesterol, terrible joint pain and fatigue. Now, I can run with my dog Oscar for up to an hour a day. With all my personal success in weight loss and my complete well-being, by this time I was determined to stay on the *Slim-It-Down Diet Smoothies* for life.

I must confess that in the past I didn't like vegetables and I thought that eating healthy was just too much work to begin with. But, my discovery of smoothies in general, coupled with my very own *Slim-It-Down Diet Smoothies* has changed all that. Now, preparing healthy meals and eating (or drinking) veggies has never been easier or tasted so good.

Since then I have also shared my special *Slim-It-Down Diet Smoothies* with some family and friends. Not only did they enjoy the recipes, but they've lost a total of over 2,000 pounds. That is why I am so passionate and inspired to help people like you lose weight and keep it off – because it works. I'm not a fitness guru, medical doctor or weight management consultant. Neither am I affiliated with any major pharmaceutical firm. But, just like you, I wanted to lose weight quickly, easily, safely and even more importantly – forever. The *Slim-It-Down Diet Smoothies* has remarkably been life-changing.

Later on in my book, I will share some essential details

about how you can further sustain your health with the *Slim-It-Down Diet Smoothies* once and for all. I am here to help you get in top shape. Cheers to better health. If you love life, you will love my *Slim-It-Down Diet Smoothies*.

ON WRITING THIS BOOK

To be frank, sharing my *Slim-It-Down Diet Smoothies* with my family and friends was easy. But, writing a book to share with others had its fair share of challenges. I had spent countless hours trying to decide the best course of action that I should take. A diet book requires great responsibility on the part of the author. They require well-founded research, experience and even more importantly they should deliver on their promise. Whilst my aim is to change lives with my *Slim-It-Down Diet Smoothies*, it can be especially hard to please every reader with one book. Particularly, when it comes to smoothies, everyone has different preferences for taste, color, fruits, vegetables, liquid base, and other additives. In some cases, there may even be allergy concerns or other health factors that may influence a reader's smoothie choices. For instance, someone may be lactose-intolerant and should stick to dairy-free smoothies while someone with diabetes should avoid smoothies that are high in calories and carbohydrates. This is why I had to find a way to strike a balance with my *Slim-It-Down Diet Smoothies* so that everyone could benefit.

In order to satisfy different reader preferences the book provides readers with smoothie recipes that can easily be tweaked to suit an individual's preference and taste. Additionally, it also provides substitute suggestions to make your whole experience even easier and more enjoyable. I fully understand that making smoothies is often an imaginative, self-expressive and exciting experience, and hence for this reason, your creativity is welcome.

I am completely aware that in the end, the possibility

exists that not everyone will like every smoothie in this book. But, my hope is that you and every other reader can find healthy and tantalizing *Slim-It-Down Diet Smoothies* that really transform your health. I also hope that you'll find recipes that you and your family will love and that you'll make them over and over again, like I do.

WHERE ARE MY BEFORE & AFTER PHOTOS?

As you may notice, I don't have any "before and after" photos in my book, and I'll tell you why. I am not some phony marketer who may hop over to Photoshop, fix some fake photos and say, "that's me". I am just sharing my knowledge, experience, research and results with millions of people like you, who are really passionate about living a healthy lifestyle.

WHY ARE THE Slim-It-Down SMOOTHIES SO EFFECTIVE IN WEIGHT LOSS?

With *Slim-It-Down Diet Smoothies* you can experience maximum weight loss results and other health benefits with little effort. The recipes in this book are the result of four years of making and testing a variety of healthy smoothies of different taste, texture, color and benefits.

It is a fact that most weight loss programs and diet pills have failed to give safe and consistent weight loss results. But, that's not the case here. Losing weight with *Slim-It-Down Diet Smoothies* is an effective and easy way to DROP pounds and inches and even more importantly – keep it off!

Unlike many so-called "healthy smoothie recipes", *Slim-It-Down Diet Smoothies* are specially tailored to fully support your fat loss efforts and avoid common smoothie mistakes.

WHAT ARE THE REWARDS OF THIS DIET?

With a regular Slim-It-Down Diet Smoothie regime, you will be able to:
- Burn fat faster while you boost your metabolism
- Curb your appetite
- Lessen bloating and water retention
- Boost the levels of your body's natural flab fighter
- Surge your body's insulin sensitivity (helps to regulate blood sugar levels)
- Improve your overall health while decreasing your risk

of diseases such as cancer, heart disease, type 2 diabetes and other ailments
- Have enhanced longevity
- Slim down and regain your confidence

HOW QUICKLY WILL I SEE RESULTS?

In most cases, you can expect to see results by the end of the first week. But, obviously everyone is different. If you are overweight you should start to see results within the first 2 weeks on the *Slim-It-Down Diet Smoothies*.

You could lose up to 10 pounds (maybe even more) in a one-month period.

WHAT TO EXPECT FROM THIS BOOK

With this book, you will get 100 healthy smoothie recipes and learn how to use smoothies to get the health results that you really want. Instead of using smoothie recipes that go against your weight loss and healthy lifestyle efforts, this book is packed with healthy smoothie recipes that are convenient and effective in burning fat (not muscles).

Slim-It-Down Diet Smoothies gives weight loss results that are:
- **FAST** – Slim-It-Down Diet can actually speed up your weight loss by boosting your metabolism.
- **EASY** – You can quickly (in less than 30 minutes) make a healthy smoothie beverage with ingredients that you can easily find in your nearest local food store and even on Amazon's website.
- **PERMANENT** – Getting into a routine of using this diet can easily give lasting results for your weight loss goals.

REALITY CHECK!

The reality is... We don't eat as correctly as we should, so we need calorie safe zones that keep us anchored while we learn how to eat correctly. *Slim-It-Down Diet Smoothies* contain nutrients that offer those safe havens. Moreover, many *Slim-It-Down Diet Smoothie* lovers find it to be convenient because they don't have to think about food, plan meals or buy many expensive products.

EXPECT A HEALTHY SMOOTHIE AND NOTHING LESS

It is true that the words "healthy smoothies" has been lightly tossed around and are sometimes nothing more than a "sugary slush". But, you can rest assured that the *Slim-It-Down Diet Smoothies* are branded as "healthy smoothies" because they truly are. This is because I've made effort to ensure they are made up of only the best recommended healthy ingredients. So you can expect nothing less.

SLIM-IT-DOWN DIET SMOOTHIES INGREDIENTS

Here's what you need to know about the Slim-It-Down Diet smoothie ingredients:

SMOOTHIE SWEETENERS

The problem that I've had with most so-called "healthy smoothies" is that they <u>DO NOT</u> contain healthy sweeteners. Research has shown that sweeteners such as refined sugar, honey, agave syrup, splenda and aspartame are not always healthy. For me, "healthy" means "healthy" and this is why I have ensured that my *Slim-It-Down Diet Smoothies* uses the safest sweeteners for optimal health.

FRUITS

Yes, even though fruits also contain sugar (fructose), it is far better for our health than processed or refined sugars. This is why fruits are the main ingredients in most of my *Slim-It-Down Diet Smoothies*. Moreover, bananas, berries and other fruits contain simple sugars for a quick energy boost plus complex carbohydrates which provide energy for hours. In this case, you won't experience the sugar crash that you get from artificial sugars or energy drinks.

DATES

Want a date? Dates are a perfect natural substitute for unhealthy sugars and this is why I've used pitted dates in some of my *Slim-It-Down Diet Smoothies*. However, you may also consider substituting 1 teaspoon organic dates sugar for 1 pitted date. For your personal taste, you may add more dates for added sweetness in your smoothies. Just be reminded that each date carries about 40-66 calories.

What are the health benefits of dates? Dates are fruits and they are an extremely rich source of dietary fiber, vitamins and minerals. In addition, studies have shown that *dates* are also effective in enhancing mental functions, maintaining healthy blood pressure, improving immune system and relieving migraine, asthma and aching muscles.

Where to buy dates? I buy my dates from Amazon because it's so convenient. You may also get it at your nearest organic food store.

SMOOTHIE BASE

By adding a liquid base or fruits with high liquidity, it will allow the solid ingredients to move around in your blender to get the right thickness and consistency.

WATER or ICE

You'll find pure filtered water or ice in some of my recipes. Water based smoothies are lower in calories, easier on your pockets and can be just as good. Ice (made with pure filtered water) is also a great choice and usually it will give your smoothie an ideal and frothy consistency.

For the recipes that contain water or ice as the smoothie base, I've added an option for protein powder. Let me explain why adding a protein powder may or may not be necessary. A good quality protein powder in smoothies has been found to reduce short-term food intake and may even help in reducing appetite. Nevertheless, if your goal is NOT to lose weight, but to live an overall healthy lifestyle, I don't think that a protein powder is always necessary. You'll learn more about the vegetarian friendly protein powder further on.

FAT-FREE YOGURT

Smoothies can turn out to be just as fattening as a fast food meal if not created correctly. Hence, in order to keep your fat intake at a minimum, some *Slim-It-Down* Diet Smoothies has fat-free yogurt. I have opted to use fat-free Greek Yogurt in my recipes because it is well known as one of the healthiest weight loss diet foods available. Furthermore, fat-free Greek Yogurt is rich in both calcium and protein, an important combination to include in any weight loss regime. This type of yogurt has about twice the amount of protein than regular plain non-fat yogurt and with about the same amount of calories. Generally, smoothies made with fat-free Greek Yogurt are normally more satisfying in terms of appetite control than regular yogurt smoothies. It also helps to further protect against "Muscle Loss Syndrome" which is basically muscle loss. Fat-free Greek Yogurt also helps to protect women from the loss of calcium that may occur whenever a woman goes on any diet plan. Note that if you prefer to go dairy-free, please consider adding a tablespoon of soaked organic chia seeds to 1 serving of smoothie instead. Chia seeds will give your smoothie consistency and the desired thickness without worrying about lactose problems. Moreover, chia seeds are proven to support weight loss and good health.

UNSWEETENED ALMOND MILK

In this book, I've used unsweetened almond milk as a liquid base for some recipes. If you prefer to use dairy for whatever reason – you may use fat-free milk. Other healthy substitutes may include pure filtered water, coconut water, and coconut milk.

What if you are allergic to nuts? In cases where nut consumption is an issue, you may opt to make your smoothie with pure filtered water or fat-free milk.

JUICE

When it comes to juices, I like to keep it freshly squeezed. I would suggest that you stay away from commercially produced juices that contain high fructose corn syrup as these additives can negatively affect blood sugar levels, digestion, among other health issues. Overall, you are not limited to what type of juice you can use – orange, apple, pineapple, cranberry, grape or others are just fine. It's your choice! If you can't get your juice freshly squeezed, you may opt for pure filtered water or coconut water.

PROTEIN ADDITIVE

As studies and experiments have shown, developing muscles can significantly contribute to your weight loss. This is because muscles help you burn calories, even while you are at rest. Unfortunately, today's modern foods make you more susceptible to a diet that's low in protein but high in carbs and fats. Hence, adding protein to your smoothies is a great way to decrease your body fat and also prevent muscle loss. Importantly, your goal is to lose fat not muscles.

By adding quality sources of protein to your smoothie, you

can turn it into a complete meal. The recommended protein powder in my *Slim-It-Down Diet Smoothies* is Garden of Life RAW Protein; however feel free to use your favorite whey protein while ensuring you use the best available protein powder. Garden of Life RAW Protein is vegan friendly, dairy-free, gluten-free and soy-free. Stay away from inferior quality sources or brands which are sometimes loaded with sugar, carbs, and chemicals. You will need the best quality natural form of protein in order to get great health benefits. Just to clear the air – I am not an affiliate of Garden of Life products. I just happened to like the product.

Furthermore, whey protein is popular among athletes for many good reasons. The benefits are almost countless when carefully evaluated. Firstly, it is highly respected as a great source of protein. In recent years, it has also caught on well with the anti-aging and longevity health groups. Why? An increasing number of studies has found that whey may potentially reduce cancer rates, fight HIV, boost immunity, reduce stress and lower cortisol, improve liver function in persons suffering from hepatitis, improve performance, reduce blood pressure and so many more health benefits.

One of the main advantages of using whey is its apparent ability to raise glutathione (GSH). The importance of GSH for the correct function of the immune system cannot be overstated. This GSH is seen as one of the most important water-soluble antioxidant found in the human body. The presence of intracellular GSH is directly related to an important part of the immune system which reacts to challenges which clearly suggest that intracellular GSH levels are one way to control the immune function. GSH is a tri-peptide which is made of amino acids L-cysteine, L-glutamine and glycine. Now, because GSH is well known in science to be vital to our immunity, oxidative stress, and our overall well-being and even due to fact that reduced levels of GSH are associated with a long list of diseases, it becomes obvious that whey has its place in a good nutrition program or diet.

OTHER IMPORTANT INGREDIENTS

Chia Seeds are a great source of fiber. It is a good idea to soak them a bit to soften them before adding them to your smoothie. Additionally, they are the richest plant source of Omega-3 and they also reduce food cravings by preventing some of the food that you eat from getting absorbed into your system too quickly. This slowing down of calorie absorption makes them a great diet helper. Therefore, they will help you to feel full easier and faster.

Goji Berries are a great way to pack antioxidants into your smoothie that will give you an extra kick of energy. It is a superfood which contains 19 amino acids – the building blocks of protein. Goji berries also contain polysaccharides which support the immune system. It be eaten raw, cooked, or dried (like raisins) and are used in herbal teas, juices, wines, and medicines. A number of researches have shown that eating berries such as blueberries, cranberries, acai berries, strawberries, cherries and other berries will offer great health benefits. Additionally, the goji berries Goji berries are rich in up to 21 trace minerals including zinc, iron, copper, calcium, germanium, selenium and phosphorus and other compounds rich in vitamin A that are great for overall health.

Flax Seed is high in omega 3 fatty acids. Just add a tablespoon of flax seed or oil and you would have had your healthy fats for the day. It is a good idea to soak them a bit for at least an hour before adding them to your smoothie.

EATING VEGGIES MADE EASY

In addition to fruits, some *smoothies* have a healthy combination of fruits and vegetables. This makes it easy to whip up a delicious array of flavors and colors, plus with added fiber, minerals and phytochemicals. Also, drinking our smoothies is an easy way to consume the much required daily fruit and veggie servings. The American Cancer Society recommends that we eat 5-9 servings of fruits and vegetables each day to prevent cancer and other diseases. Yet many of us hate vegetables and rarely eat them or eat enough. One great advantage of the *Slim-It-Down Diet Smoothies* is that you can hide the taste of your veggies by embedding them in the smoothies.

Moreover, these *smoothies* are designed ideally between 100 and 350 calories. With these calorie-controlled smoothies, dieters will feel full and will be able to keep hunger at bay while improving recommended nutritional intake.

CHOOSING SMOOTHIE SUBSTITUTIONS

Slim-It-Down Smoothies can be easily tweaked to suit your personal preferences and to bring your wildest imagination alive. Also, wherever you see recipes for 2 servings, you may cut the recipe in half for 1 serving.

Here are some listed smoothie substitute ingredient suggestions:

- Substitute **water** for: fat-free milk, unsweetened almond milk or unsweetened coconut water
- Substitute **mango** for : papaya or pineapple
- Substitute **banana** for: avocado
- Substitute **cantaloupe** for: honeydew, papaya, apple or pear
- Substitute **strawberries** for: raspberries or cherries
- Substitute **blueberries** for blackberries
- Substitute **kale** for spinach

BOOSTING YOUR METABOLISM WITH THE Slim-It-Down DIET SMOOTHIES

Simply put, metabolism is a process which converts the food that we eat into energy. This converted energy is then used to provide fuel to the cells in our bodies. Using *Slim-It-Down Diet Smoothies* is a great way to boost your metabolism. These smoothies are an easy and healthy way to maximize your efforts to get in shape and stay in shape.

So here's the deal, weight loss occurs when your metabolism gets moving and you put out more calories than you take in. Let's do the math:

If you were to replace your usual 800-calorie meal with a *Slim-It-Down Diet* 300-calorie smoothie, you'd have saved 500 calories per day. In no time, you'd start to see and feel the results.

So what's the connection here? By increasing your energy levels, you will be able to increase your activity and automatically burn more calories. **Burn more calories – lose more weight!**

HOW THE Slim-It-Down DIET WORKS

Using these diet smoothies will vary depending on your health goals. The two recommended ways that you can use *The Slim-It-Down Diet Smoothies* are:
1. The Optimal Health Approach
2. The Weight Loss Approach

1. THE OPTIMAL HEALTH APPROACH

By having healthy smoothies to optimize your health, your body will love you even more. *The Optimal Health Approach* is perfect if you want to maintain your current weight or live a healthy lifestyle. With this approach, instead of having your usual breakfast menu, substitute your breakfast for a eight (8) ounce glass of nutritionally balanced *Slim-It-Down Diet* smoothie.

Not in the mood for substituting your usual breakfast? How about substituting lunch or maybe even dinner? Give yourself an energy boost by indulging in your favorite *Slim-It-Down Diet* smoothie sometime around midday or dinner-time. By drinking a nutrient-rich, low-calorie *Slim-It-Down Diet* smoothie it will help to give you more appetite control and make it easier to cut back on regular suppertime meal proportions. Say goodbye to regular hunger pangs.

In addition, you can replace your usual snack with an 8 ounce glass of your favorite Slim-It-Down Diet smoothie, whenever you wish. Snacking works particularly great if you prepare your favorite smoothie ahead of time and sip it whenever you have that sugar or snack craving. Happy snacking! This is healthy and delicious snacking at its best.

Continue this regime for as long as you'd like and remember to rotate your smoothies (variety is the spice of life).

2. WEIGHT LOSS APPROACH

Using Slim-It-Down Diet Smoothies for weight loss is easy and gives dieters much flexibility with 2 simple steps.

<u>Step One:</u> *Smoothie Fasting Day*

From both a scientific and historic standpoint, fasting is nothing new. In fact, modern science has uncovered evidence that fasting supports our well-being in more ways than one. As some research suggests, fasting may increase longevity, reduce levels of IGF-1 (Insulin-Like Growth Factor 1, an issue which leads to fast-tracked aging), lower the risk of certain cancers and risk of heart disease, reduce high blood pressure, blood sugar and cholesterol levels and activate DNA repair genes.

For the *Smoothie Fasting Day,* on one (1) day each week

you will refrain from all other meals and indulge in healthy energizing and satisfying *Slim-It-Down Diet Smoothies* all day. This will help to accelerate your metabolism each week so that you lose at least 2 to 6 pounds per week.

How much should you have on your *Smoothie Fasting Day*?

I recommend that dieters consume no more than 2 quarts (64 ounces) of smoothies per day. I must emphasize that this doesn't mean you have to have 2 quarts. Just drink enough to keep you full enough. Additionally, you should pay attention to the calories intake per serving.

IMPORTANTLY, in order to further support your fat loss efforts on your *Smoothie Fasting Day*, I recommend that you choose at least 2-3 servings of Slim-It-Down Diet Smoothies that contain protein powder or Greek Yogurt. These servings should be spread evenly throughout the day. Ideally, you should have one in the morning, midday and then another for dinner. This will help to further curb your appetite for longer hours throughout the entire day.

Give yourself the best possible chance of success by choosing your fasting day in advance and based on your particular lifestyle. Feel free to choose a different day each week, but just remember that you should stick to your easiest and best possible option.

Step Two: 6-Day Energy Giver

The *Smoothie Fasting Day* is followed by the **6-Day Energy Giver.** For the *6-Day Energy Giver* (the other 6 days of the week) you can eat normally **balanced meals** WITHOUT counting calories. Just do NOT overeat! Overeating can ruin any diet plan. You should always stop eating when you're full.

You should continue to do your *Smoothie Fasting Day* and the *6-Day Energy Giver* until you've reached your targeted weight. After reaching this target, you should switch to the "The

Optimal Health Approach" on a daily basis for a lifestyle of optimum health.

How to take an effective approach?

It is best to cycle your *Slim-It-Down Smoothies*. This simply means that you do not drink the same smoothie over and over every day. For example, you could do a recipe that contains spinach one day, romaine lettuce the next, and kale on the third.

GETTING THE MOST OUT OF EACH SMOOTHIE

Ever since my invention of the *Slim-It-Down Diet Smoothies*, I have been drinking them daily myself and sharing them with others. As mentioned earlier, everyone in my family fell in love with them and many of my friends did too.

To help you get the most benefits from drinking *Slim-It-Down Diet Smoothies* and to avoid some typical mistakes, I'll share some personal guidelines:

- To make my smoothie routine much easier, I usually prepare my smoothie first thing in the morning in the amount that I usually consume in one day. My usual consumption amount per day does not exceed 1.5 quarts (48 ounces). This works out to be about 6 glasses (8-oz glass). On the contrary, if 8 glasses per day is what works for you, it is still okay.
- After pouring enough smoothies in a glass for my morning satisfaction I store the rest in my refrigerator. I will usually have to shake it well when I am ready to drink it as separation of the juices and fiber in the fruit usually occurs.
- I sip my smoothie slowly. Sometimes I even put my smoothie in a coffee mug with a lid and carry it with me to the car or to my office. This is a cute way of minimizing any chance of spilling it and keeping it private.
- I never drink my smoothies with a meal. Not even with a candy.

- I don't eat anything approximately 35 minutes before or 35 minutes after I've finished my smoothie. This is to ensure that I get the most nutritional benefit out of each smoothie.
- If I decide to add more ingredients to my smoothie, I try to keep it simple in order to maximize nutritional benefits and to keep it easy on my digestive system.
- I stick to my favorite *Slim-It-Down Diet Smoothies* (yes, I have favorites) so that I am always looking forward to the next one. Taste appeals to everyone differently, so it is almost natural that you'll come up with your own favorite list of smoothies.
- Particularly for green smoothies, I always rotate the green leaves that I add to my smoothies. This is because almost all greens in the world contain minute amounts of alkaloids. Note that tiny quantities of alkaloids will not cause you any harm and may even strengthen your immune system. Nevertheless, if you continue to consume kale, or spinach, or any other single greens for many weeks without rotating it, eventually it is possible that the same type of alkaloids can accumulate in your body and cause unwanted symptoms. Please note that you don't have to rotate the fruit in your green smoothies, just rotate the greens.
- I choose organic produce whenever I go shopping. This is most important because consuming organic food gives superior nutrition in comparison to conventionally grown produce.
- I never over drink. Whenever I am full, that's the time I stop drinking.
- I usually do my *Smoothie Fasting Day* on a day that I will be at home. If I really have to be somewhere else, I will make my smoothie ahead of time and store it in a portable cold storage container.
- I don't use left-over smoothies unless it was kept in sealed container.

SMOOTHIE STORAGE FOR BUSY PEOPLE

Can you store your smoothies if you are busy? Yes, you can make your smoothies ahead of time. You can freeze a smoothie and thaw it out when you want it. You'll need to allow some space in the container because your smoothie will likely expand when freezing.

Bear in mind that your aim is to have your smoothies as fresh as possible. Consequently, you should only practice smoothie storage if you must.

You may keep any excess smoothie in a sealed container in your refrigerator and consume the remaining portion for lunch or dinner. You can prepare your smoothie ahead of time and have it ready the next morning. Be sure to shake it well when you are ready to drink it as separation of the juices and fiber in the fruit will occur.

GENERAL STEPS TO MAKE THE BEST SMOOTHIES

Even though these smoothies are quick and easy to make, here are 5 steps that will help you to make the best smoothies every time:

Step 1: Add the liquid in your blender first. It is best to use a little less than what may be necessary and then add extra afterwards.

Step 2: Add all of the fruits and vegetables that you want to include in the smoothie.

Step 3: Add anything extra to the smoothie for added flavorings, added nutrition or to change the consistency. These are your healthy smoothie additives. Choosing the right healthy additive is important for many reasons.

Step 4: Add whole or crushed ice to the smoothie to help get the consistency to what you like. Note that depending on whether you are using frozen or fresh veggies and fruits, you will need to add more or less ice.

Step 5: Blend all ingredients together to make your smoothie. Usually it is good to pulse the blender a little until things get fairly mixed up, and then let the blender liquefy everything until it is smooth and gives the desired consistency that. At this point add more ice to make it thicker and more liquid to make it thinner. Pour and enjoy!

LET'S GET STARTED

I have spent a lot of time to bring these recipes to perfection, but sometimes it's impossible to catch it all. So, if you see any glaring errors made in this book, please send me an email at: dianesharpe@weightlosspeeps.com. I will be very grateful for your feedback and I will make the changes as quickly as possible.

Let's kick-start your health and wellness smoothie regime by exploring a wholesome variety of smoothies. Try one of my favorite recipes: the *Sizzling Watermelon Smoothie* – it tastes great! Also, in order to further support your weight loss goals; please see the essential diet tips.

Live a healthier life and lose weight with *Slim-It-Down Diet Smoothies* – it works.

BREAKFAST ENERGY SMOOTHIES

A Quick Note: Start your day with one of these *Slim-It-Down Diet* breakfast smoothies. Setting apart 10-20 minutes every morning to make your favorite smoothie is probably the best time you'll ever invest in your life. As a daily routine, these breakfast smoothies provides a nutritious and fulfilling treat to keep you hydrated and provide you with a feeling of well-being all day long.

Wondering if you can have these smoothies outside of breakfast? Sure, you can. You can have any Slim-It-Down Diet Smoothie any time of day. But, if you aren't sure what to have for breakfast, the "Breakfast Energy Smoothies" are my best picks.

Orange 'n' Berries Smoothie

Preparation Time: *15 Minutes*
Calories: *201*
Servings: *1*

Ingredients
¼ cup Orange Juice
½ cup Blueberries
1 cup Strawberries; hulled
½ cup fat-free plain Greek Yogurt

Directions:
Place all ingredients into your blender and process until smooth or for about a minute. Pour in a glass and serve.

Oat 'n' Peach Smoothie

Preparation Time: *15 Minutes*
Calories: *165 per serving*
Servings: 2

Ingredients:
2 ½ cups of Water
3 tablespoons Rolled Oats
1 very Ripe Peach, pitted and chopped
2 Pitted Dates
¼ cup freshly squeezed Orange Juice
2 tablespoons Protein Powder (recommended - Garden of Life RAW Protein)

Directions:
In a saucepan, add the water and oats and bring to a boil; then reduce the heat and simmer for 3 minutes.
Remove the cooked oats from the heat and let it cool.
Place the cooled oat mixture in your blender and process until smooth, and then add the remaining ingredients. Process again until very smooth.
Note: Feel free to use your preferred Protein Mix.

Banana Blues Smoothie

Preparation Time: *15 Minutes*
Calories: *290*
Serving: *1*

Ingredients:
1 cup Frozen Organic Blueberries
1 Ripe Banana, sliced
1 cup Fat-Free Plain Greek Yogurt

Directions:
In a blender, combine banana, blueberries, and yogurt and blend on high speed until smooth. Serve and enjoy.

Power-up Pomegranate Smoothie

Preparation Time: *15 Minutes*
Calories: *224 per serving*
Serving: *1*

Ingredients:
¼ cup Pomegranate Juice, freshly squeezed
1 cup Cantaloupe, chopped into chunks
½ tablespoon fresh Lime Juice
1 teaspoon Natural Almond Oil /Almond Essence
1 slice fresh Ginger (optional)
2 Pitted Dates or 1 teaspoon Dates Sugar

Directions:
Combine all ingredients in a blender and mix until smooth. Add more water if needed. Serve and enjoy.

Energizing Morning Smoothie

Preparation Time: *15 Minutes*
Calories: *272*
Serving: *1*

Ingredients:
¾ cup Orange Juice
¾ cup fat-free plain Greek Yogurt
½ of a medium Papaya - peeled, seeds removed and sliced
1 teaspoon Lime Juice
½ Ripe Banana, sliced
3 Ice Cubes

Directions:
Place all ingredients into your blender and process until smooth. Pour in a glass and serve.

Tangy Raspberry Smoothie

Preparation Time: *15 Minutes*
Calories: *230*
Serving: *1*

Ingredients:
½ cup fresh Raspberries
¼ cup freshly squeezed Orange Juice
½ cup fat-free plain Greek Yogurt
2 pitted Dates

Directions:
Place all ingredients into your blender and process until smooth or for about a minute. Pour in a glass and serve.

So Good Coffee Smoothie

Preparation Time: *15 Minutes*
Calories: *190 per serving*
Serving: *2*

Ingredients:
1 cup unsweetened Almond Milk
2 tablespoons Protein Powder (recommended - Garden of Life RAW Protein)
¾ cup Black Coffee (use your favorite coffee (decaf or regular)
2 medium ripe Bananas, sliced
1 cup Ice Cubes

Directions:
Place all ingredients into your blender and process until smooth or for about a minute. Pour in a glass and serve.

Zesty Papaya Smoothie

Preparation Time: *15 Minutes*
Calories: *220*
Servings: *1*

Ingredients
1 cup Papaya, peeled, pitted & chopped
1 cup unsweetened Almond Milk
1 small Lime or Lemon, juiced
½ cup fat-free plain Greek Yogurt

Directions:
Place all ingredients into your blender and process until smooth or for about a minute. Pour in a glass and serve.

Almond Vanilla Comforting Smoothie

Preparation Time: *15 Minutes*
Calories: *267 per serving*
Serving: *2*

Ingredients:
1 teaspoon Nutmeg
1 teaspoon Vanilla Extract
2 pitted Dates (optional)
¼ cup Ground Almonds
2 Ripe Bananas (frozen works best)
½ cup fat free Vanilla Greek Yogurt
¼ cup brewed and chilled Chamomile tea
¼ cup unsweetened Almond Milk
3-4 Ice Cubes

Directions:
Place all the ingredients into your high-speed blender and blend until nice and smooth. Serve and enjoy.

Low-fat Mango Smoothie

Preparation Time: *15 Minutes*
Calories: *165*
Serving: *1*

Ingredients:
1 medium ripe Mango - peeled, pitted, chopped
¾ cup unsweetened Almond Milk (cold)
¼ cup fat-free vanilla Greek Yogurt
¾ teaspoon Vanilla Extract
2 Ice Cubes
Pinch of Salt (optional)

Directions:
Place all ingredients into your blender and process until smooth. Pour into your glass and serve.

Greek Apple Smoothie

Preparation Time: *15 Minutes*
Calories: *235 per serving*
Serving: *2*

Ingredients:
1 medium ripe Bananas, sliced
2 medium Apples, peeled, cored and quartered
1 cup fat-free plain Greek Yogurt
2 Pitted Dates (optional)
1½ cups unsweetened Almond Milk

Directions:
Place all ingredients into your blender and process until smooth or for about a minute. Pour into your glass and serve.

Power-Up Banana Smoothie

Preparation Time: *15 Minutes*
Calories: 136 per serving
Servings: 2

Ingredients
1 medium ripe Banana, frozen and sliced
½ cup unsweetened Almond Milk
¼ cup fat-free plain Greek Yogurt (optional)
1 teaspoon Flax Seed Powder
2 Walnuts
5 cubes of ice

Directions:
Place all ingredients into your blender and process until silky smooth. Pour in your glass and serve.

Orangey Date Smoothie

Preparation Time: *15 Minutes*
Calories: *310*
Servings: *1*

Ingredients:
4 dried Dates, pitted
Zest and juice of 2 Oranges
1 cup fat-free plain Greek yogurt

Directions:
Place all ingredients into your blender and process until smooth. Pour into your glass and serve.

Yummy Almond Butter Smoothie

Preparation Time: *15 Minutes*
Calories: *236*
Serving: *1*

Ingredients:
1 cup unsweetened Almond Milk
1/3 ripe Banana, sliced
1 tablespoon Almond Butter (use homemade or without additives)
2 pitted Dates (optional)
4 Ice Cubes

Directions:
Place milk, banana, almond butter and dates into your blender and process until smooth. Add ice cubes and pulse. Pour in your glass and enjoy.

Oats Blend Smoothie

Preparation Time: *15 Minutes*
Serving: *2*
Calories: *156 per serving*

Ingredients:
¾ cup unsweetened Almond Milk
1 teaspoon Vanilla Extract
½ cup fat-free plain Greek Yogurt
¼ cup Quick-cook Oats
1 tablespoon Ground Flaxseed
1 teaspoon Unsweetened Cocoa Powder
1 teaspoon Ground Cinnamon
1 small ripe Banana (frozen works best)

Directions:
Place all the ingredients into your high-speed blender and blend until it is smooth enough to drink. Enjoy!

Classic Strawberry 'n' Banana Smoothie

Preparation Time: *15 Minutes*
Servings: *2*
Calories: *235 per serving*

Ingredients
6 large Strawberries
1 Ripe Banana (frozen & sliced)
1 cup of unsweetened Almond Milk

Directions:
Place all ingredients into your blender and process until smooth. Pour in a glass and enjoy.

Pumpkin Bliss Smoothie

Preparation Time: *15 Minutes*
Calories: *171 per serving*
Serves: *2*

Ingredients:
1 cup unsweetened Almond Milk
¼ cup Rolled Whole Oats
¼ cup organic pureed Canned Pumpkin (or make your own pureed pumpkin)
1 tablespoon Whole Chia Seeds, pre-soaked in water
½ frozen Ripe Banana
1 teaspoon Cinnamon
2 pitted Dates
3 Ice Cubes

Note: Chia Seeds should be taken from the soaked water for blending.

Directions:
Place all the ingredients into your high-speed blender and

blend until nice and smooth. Serve and enjoy.

Kiwi 'n' Citrus Mix Smoothie

Preparation Time: *15 Minutes*
Calories: *187 per serving*
Servings: *2*

Ingredients
1 Ripe Banana, peeled and sliced
1 large Orange, peeled and pitted
1 large Kiwi Fruit, peeled and chopped
½ cup plus 2 tablespoons freshly squeezed Orange Juice
½ cup plus 2 tablespoons Grapefruit Juice

Directions:
Place all ingredients into your blender and process until smooth or for about a minute. Pour in a glass and serve.

Oat Dream Smoothie

Preparation Time: *15 Minutes*
Calories: *315*
Serving: *1*

Ingredients:
½ cup fat-free Plain Greek Yogurt
½ cup unsweetened Almond Milk
1 ripe Banana, sliced
¼ cup Old-Fashioned Rolled Oats
2 pitted Dates
1 cup Ice Cups

Directions:
Combine all your ingredients in your blender and blend until it is it gives a smooth look. Enjoy!

Berries & Cinnamon Smoothie

Preparation Time: *15 Minutes*
Calories: *235 per serving*
Servings: *2*

Ingredients
1 cup unsweetened Almond Milk
½ cup fresh Strawberries
½ medium ripe Mango, cut into chunks
½ cup frozen Blueberries
¼ cup frozen Raspberries
½ cup Cantaloupe, cut into chunks
1 ripe Banana, sliced
1 large Carrot (7-1/4" to 8-1/2" long), sliced thinly
Dash of Cinnamon

Directions:
Place all ingredients into your blender and process until smooth or for about a minute. Pour in a glass and serve.

GREEN BOOST SMOOTHIES

A Quick Note: These *Slim-It-Down* Green Smoothies are perfect to have any time of day and even for detox. Note that for detox purposes you do not need to add protein powder. These Green Smoothies contains a delicious and balanced blend of fruits and vegetables and is great way to "hide your veggies" in your drink. Additionally, *Slim-It-Down* Green Smoothies provide the nutrition, vitamins, minerals, healthy carbs, fiber and low fat whole food that you need to lose weight quickly, safely and effectively without starving yourself.

Amazing Apricot Smoothie

Preparation Time: *15 Minutes*
Calories: *127 per serving*
Serving: *2*

Ingredients:
2 cups Water
1 cup Apricots
1 ripe Banana
1 cup Romaine Lettuce
2 tablespoons Protein Powder, recommended - Garden of Life
RAW Protein (optional)

Directions:
Place all ingredients into your blender and process until smooth or for about a minute. Pour in a glass and serve.

Raspberry Prize Smoothie

Preparation Time: *15 Minutes*
Calories: *165 per serving*
Serving: *2*

Ingredients:
2 cups Water
1 cup Raspberries
1 Banana
1 cup Pak Choi
2 tablespoons Protein Powder, recommended - Garden of Life
RAW Protein (optional)

Directions:
Place all ingredients into your blender and process until smooth or for about a minute. Pour in a glass and serve.

Tasty Spinach Smoothie

Preparation Time: *15 Minutes*
Calories: *128 per serving*
Serving: *2*

Ingredients:
2 cups Water
1 cup Strawberries
1 medium Mango
1 cup Spinach
2 tablespoons Protein Powder, recommended - Garden of Life
RAW Protein (optional)

Directions:
Place all ingredients into your blender and process until smooth or for about a minute. Pour in a glass and serve.

Blueberry Paradise Smoothie

Preparation Time: *15 Minutes*
Calories: *144 per serving*
Serving: *2*

Ingredients:
2 cups Water
1 cup Blueberries
1 Banana
1 cup Spinach
2 tablespoons Protein Powder, recommended - Garden of Life RAW Protein (optional)

Directions:
Place all ingredients into your blender and process until smooth or for about a minute. Pour in a glass and serve.

Beginner's Green Smoothie

Preparation Time: *15 Minutes*
Calories: *284*
Serving: *1*

Ingredients:
1 cup Water
2 Apples – peeled, cored, chopped
1 Banana
½ Cucumber (medium), chopped

Directions:
Place all ingredients into your blender and process until smooth or for about a minute. Pour in a glass and serve.

Energizing Tropical Smoothie

Preparation Time: *15 Minutes*
Calories: *140 per serving*
Serving: *2*

Ingredients:
2 cups Water
1 cup Pineapple
1 ripe Banana, sliced
1 cup Spinach
2 tablespoons Protein Powder, recommended - Garden of Life
RAW Protein (optional)

Directions:
Place all ingredients into your blender and process until smooth or for about a minute. Pour in a glass and serve.

Strawberry & Greens Smoothie

Preparation Time: *15 Minutes*
Servings: *2*
Calories: *143 per serving*

Ingredients:
½ Ripe Banana, sliced
6 large Strawberries
2 cups Spinach
1 large Orange, peeled and sliced
1/3 cup fat-free plain Greek Yogurt
1 cup ice (optional based on preference)

Directions:
Put all ingredients into a blender and blend until smooth.

Amazing Celery Smoothie

Preparation Time: *15 Minutes*
Calories: *320 per serving*
Serving: *1*

Ingredients:
1 cup Water
3 Peaches, peeled, sliced
1 ripe Banana, sliced
2 Celery Stalks
2 tablespoons Protein Powder, recommended - Garden of Life RAW Protein (optional)

Directions:
Place all ingredients into your blender and process until smooth or for about a minute. Pour in a glass and serve.

Berry Twist Smoothie

Preparation Time: *15 Minutes*
Calories: *148 per serving*
Serving: *2*

Ingredients:
2 cups Water
1 cup mixed Berries – use your favorite berries
1 Mango (medium)
1 cup Spinach
2 tablespoons Protein Powder, recommended - Garden of Life
RAW Protein (optional)

Directions:
Place all ingredients into your blender and process until
smooth or for about a minute. Pour in a glass and serve.

Celery Berry Smoothie

Preparation Time: *15 Minutes*
Calories: *108 per serving*
Serving: *2*

Ingredients:
2 Celery Stalks, finely chopped
1 cup Blueberries, fresh or frozen
1½ cups unsweetened Almond Milk
½ cup of Ice

Directions:
Place all the ingredients into your high-speed blender and blend until nice and smooth. Serve and enjoy.

Go Green Smoothie

Preparation Time: *15 Minutes*
Calories: *134 per serving*
Serving: *2*

Ingredients:
1 cup Coconut Water (or Water)
1 ripe Mango (medium), peeled, seed removed and cut into chunks (or use your favorite tropical fruit)
1 cup Spinach
1 teaspoon Chia Seeds, pre-soaked in water
1 cup Parsley
1 stalk of Celery
½ cup Ice Cubes

Directions:
Place all ingredients into your blender and process until smooth. Pour in a glass and serve.

Kale Surprise Smoothie

Preparation Time: *15 Minutes*
Calories: *167 per serving*
Serving: *2*

Ingredients:
1 cup Water
2 Bananas
1 cup Kale
2 tablespoons Protein Powder, recommended - Garden of Life RAW Protein (optional)

Directions:
Place all ingredients into your blender and process until smooth or for about a minute. Pour in a glass and serve.

Delightful Lettuce Smoothie

Preparation Time: *15 Minutes*
Calories: *88 per serving*
Serving: *2*

Ingredients:
1 cup Water
1 cup Strawberries
1 ripe Banana, sliced
1 cup Romaine Lettuce

Directions:
Place all ingredients into your blender and process until smooth or for about a minute. Pour in a glass and serve.

Healthy Pear Smoothie

Preparation Time: *15 Minutes*
Calories: *192 per serving*
Serving: *2*

Ingredients:
2 cups Water
2 Pears, peeled and sliced
1 Banana, sliced
1 cup Spinach
2 tablespoons Protein Powder, recommended - Garden of Life
RAW Protein (optional)

Directions:
Place all ingredients into your blender and process until smooth or for about a minute. Pour in a glass and serve.

Mango Vibes Smoothie

Preparation Time: *15 Minutes*
Calories: *155 per serving*
Serving: *2*

Ingredients:
2 cups Water
2 large ripe Mangoes, peeled, sliced and seeds removed
1 cup Spinach
2 tablespoons Protein Powder, recommended - Garden of Life
RAW Protein (optional)

Directions:
Place all ingredients into your blender and process until smooth or for about a minute. Pour in your glass and serve.

SUPERFOOD SMOOTHIES

A Quick Note: The *Slim-It-Down* Superfood Smoothies are delicious, full of energy, vitality and most importantly – highly nutritious. These smoothies are considered great any time of day.

Goji Blast Smoothie

Preparation Time: *15 Minutes*
Calories: *282 per serving*
Serving: *2*

Ingredients:
2 cups Almond Milk
1½ cups frozen sliced Banana
1 cup frozen Strawberries
¼ cup Goji Berries (soaked overnight)
2 tablespoons Whole Flax Seed
¼ teaspoon Cinnamon

Directions:
Combine all ingredients in a blender and mix until smooth. Add more water if needed. Serve and enjoy.

Acai Berry Goodness Smoothie

Preparation Time: *15 Minutes*
Calories: *220 per serving*
Serving: *2*

Ingredients:
1 cup Acai Berry Juice
1 cup Grapes
1 cup frozen Mixed Berries (use your favorite berries)
1 cup fat-free vanilla Greek Yogurt
1 tablespoon Chia seeds, pre-soaked in water

Directions:
Place all your ingredients into the blender and process until smooth. Pour in a glass and serve.

Green Cinnamon Smoothie

Preparation Time: *15 Minutes*
Calories: *229 per serving*
Serving: *2*

Ingredients:
1 cup Spinach
3 Kale leaves chopped
2 cups unsweetened Almond Milk
2 ripe Bananas
4 tablespoon Goji Berries
1 teaspoon Vanilla Extract
2 teaspoons Cinnamon
Add ice if desired

Directions:
Add all ingredients in a blender and blend until smooth. Serves
and enjoy.

Raspberry Protein Smoothie

Preparation Time: *15 Minutes*
Calories: *275*
Serving: *1*

Ingredients:
¾ cup fat-free plain Greek Yogurt (use your favorite flavor)
½ cup of frozen Raspberries
2 pitted Dates

Directions:
Place all your ingredients into the blender and process until smooth or for about a minute. Pour in a glass and serve.

Power Berry Smoothie

Preparation Time: *15 Minutes*
Calories: *238 per serving*
Serving: *2*

Ingredients:
1 cup Fat-Free Plain Greek Yogurt
½ cup Unsweetened Almond Milk
2 small Ripe Bananas, peeled
1 tablespoon Cocoa Powder (or Fat-Free Chocolate Syrup)
1/3 cup Goji Berries
1 cup Red Grapes
2 cups (or large handfuls) of Fresh Baby Spinach
½ cup Frozen Strawberries
Water if needed

Directions:
In a blender, add the almond milk and Greek yogurt first, followed by the bananas, red grapes, frozen blueberries, soaked goji berries, baby spinach, chocolate syrup or cocoa powder. Blend on high speed for 30 seconds or until the smoothie is creamy. Add a little water (or more fat-free milk) to suit your desired consistency.

Choco Berry Smoothie

Preparation Time: *15 Minutes*
Calories: *151 per serving*
Serving: *2*

Ingredients:
1½ cups Unsweetened Almond Milk
1½ tablespoons Cocoa Powder
1 teaspoon Cinnamon
1 ripe Banana (medium), sliced
½ cup fresh or frozen Berries (use your favorite berries)
2 pitted Dates
2 tablespoons Protein Powder, recommended - Garden of Life RAW Protein (optional)

Directions:
Place all your ingredients into your high-speed blender and blend until nice and smooth. Serve and enjoy.

Creamy Choco Almond Butter Smoothie

Preparation Time: *15 Minutes*
Calories: *196 per serving*
Serving: *2*

Ingredients:
1 tablespoon creamy Almond Butter (use homemade or without additives)
1 cup fat-free plain Greek Yogurt
½ cup Unsweetened Almond Milk
1 tablespoon fat-free Cocoa Powder
1 ripe Banana, sliced

Directions:
Place all your ingredients into the blender and process until smooth. Pour in a glass and serve.

Super Power Smoothie

Preparation Time: *15 Minutes*
Calories: *168 per serving*
Serving: *2*

Ingredients:
1 cup Unsweetened Almond Milk
½ frozen large ripe Banana
1 tablespoon Cocoa Powder
1 tablespoon Chia Seeds, pre-soaked in water
2 tablespoons Goji Berries
1 teaspoon Cinnamon
4 Ice Cubes

Directions:
Combine all ingredients in your blender and process until it is smooth. Serve and enjoy.

Sweet Potato Cheers Smoothie

Preparation Time: *15 Minutes*
Calories: *360*
Serving: *1*

Ingredients:
¾ cup Unsweetened Almond Milk
¾ cup Sweet Potato, cooked and chilled
1 teaspoon Ginger, freshly grated
1 cup ripe Bananas, frozen and sliced
1 teaspoon ground Cinnamon
¼ teaspoon Nutmeg

Directions:
Place almond milk in blender first, followed by ginger, bananas, sweet potatoes, cinnamon, and nutmeg. Blend until smooth. Pour into glass and serve.

Youthful Energy Smoothie

Preparation Time*: 15 Minutes*
Calories*: 164 per serving*
Serving*: 2*

Ingredients:
½ cup fat-free plain Greek Yogurt
½ cup freshly squeezed Orange Juice
½ medium Banana, sliced
1 cup frozen Strawberries
2 tablespoon Chia Seeds

Directions:
Combine all ingredients in a blender and mix until smooth. Add more water if needed. Serve and enjoy.

Tropical Kiwi Smoothie

Preparation Time: *15 Minutes*
Calories: *378*
Serving: *1*

Ingredients:
3 Kiwi, peeled and sliced
1 cup frozen Banana slices
3/4 cup Pineapple Juice
1/2 cup frozen Strawberries

Directions:
Place all your ingredients into the blender and process until smooth or for about a minute. Pour in a glass and serve.

Low Calorie Green Smoothie

Preparation Time: *15 Minutes*
Servings: *2*
Calories: *78 per serving*

Ingredients
½ cup fat free Milk or unsweetened Almond Milk
½ medium ripe Banana (frozen – optional), sliced
1 cup fresh Spinach
1 Kiwi, sliced

Directions:
Place all your ingredients into the blender and process until smooth enough. Pour in a glass and serve.

Blackberry Tropics Smoothie

Preparation Time: *15 Minutes*
Calories: *250 per serving*
Serving: *2*

Ingredients:
1 cup Blackberries
¼ large Pineapple, core removed and cubed
1 Kiwi Fruit, peeled
1 ripe Banana, sliced
½ Pear chopped
½ cup Coconut Water (or Water)
1 tablespoon Flax Seed Oil (optional)
4 Ice Cubes

Directions:
Place all your ingredients into your high-speed blender and blend until nice and smooth. Serve and enjoy.

Berry Blast Fat-Burner Smoothie

Preparation Time: *15 Minutes*
Calories: *98 per serving*
Servings: *2*

Ingredients:
¼ cup organic Apple Juice
1 tablespoon Aloe Vera Juice
¼ cup Strawberries
¼ cup Raspberries
¼ cup Blueberries
¼ cup fresh Cranberries
1 teaspoon Ginger Root, grated
2 tablespoons Protein Powder, recommended - Garden of Life
RAW Protein (optional)

Directions:
Place all your ingredients into your blender and process until smooth or for about a minute. Pour in a glass and serve.

Greek Cranberry Smoothie

Preparation Time: *15 Minutes*
Calories: *123 per serving*
Servings: *2*

Ingredients:
2 cups frozen Cranberries
2 pitted Dates
1 cup fat-free plain Greek Yogurt

Directions:
Place all your ingredients into the blender and process until smooth or for about a minute. Pour in a glass and serve.

Shades of Red Smoothie

Preparation Time: *15 Minutes*
Calories: *233 per serving*
Serving: *2*

Ingredients:
¼ cup Raspberries
5 large Strawberries, hulled
¼ cup dried Cranberries
1 small Red Apple, cored
1 pitted Date (optional)
1¼ cups Unsweetened Almond Milk or water (add more where necessary)

Directions:
Place all your ingredients into the high-speed blender and blend until nice and smooth. Serve and enjoy.

Blueberry 'n' Banana Breeze Smoothie

Preparation Time: *15 Minutes*
Calories: *344*
Servings: *1*

Ingredients:
1 cup fresh or frozen Blueberries
1 large ripe Banana, peeled and chopped
¼ teaspoon Lemon Juice
1 cup fat-free plain Greek Yogurt
1 tablespoon Wheat Germ (optional)
2 Pitted Dates

Directions:
Place all your ingredients into the blender and process until smooth or for about a minute. Pour in a glass and serve.

Cherry Berry Smoothie

Preparation Time: *15 Minutes*
Calories: *219 per serving*
Serving: *2*

Ingredients:
1½ cups Frozen Blueberries
¾ cup Frozen Cherries
1 Ripe Banana, peeled
1 cup Fat-Free Plain Greek Yogurt
¼ cup Water
4 Ice Cubes
¼ teaspoon Vanilla Extract
2 pitted Dates (optional)

Directions:
Add all your ingredients in a blender and blend until smooth.
Serves and enjoy.

Flat Belly Blueberry Smoothie

Preparation Time: *15 Minutes*
Calories: *197 per serving*
Serving: *2*

Ingredients:
1 cup Unsweetened Almond Milk
½ cup fat-free vanilla Greek Yogurt
1½ cup fresh Blueberries
1 tablespoon Flaxseed Oil
½ cup Frozen blackberries

Directions:
Place all your ingredients into the blender and process until smooth. Pour in your glass and serve.

Flat Tummy Smoothie

Preparation Time: *15 Minutes*
Calories: *119 per serving*
Serving: *2*

Ingredients:
1 tablespoon Ground Flaxseed
1 cup Frozen Blueberries
¾ cup Unsweetened Almond Milk
½ cup fat-free plain Greek Yogurt

Directions:
Place all your ingredients into your high-speed blender and blend until nice and smooth. Serve and enjoy.

Greek Green Smoothie

Preparation Time: *15 Minutes*
Calories: *267 per serving*
Serving: *2*

Ingredients:
6 large Strawberries, (fresh, not frozen)
1 Orange, peeled and sliced
1 medium ripe Banana, peeled and chopped
2 cups Spinach
½ cup fat-free plain Greek Yogurt
¾ cup Ice (optional based on your preference)

Directions:
Place the strawberries, orange slices, banana and spinach into a blender and process for about 30 seconds.
Add the yogurt and ice and process once again until smooth. Pour into glasses and serve.

Blackberry Protein Smoothie

Preparation Time: *15 Minutes*
Calories: *180*
Serving: *1*

Ingredients:
2 teaspoon Vanilla Extract
½ cup Blackberries
1 cup Unsweetened Almond Milk
2 tablespoons Protein Powder, recommended - Garden of Life RAW Protein (optional)
3 Ice Cubes

Directions:
Place all your ingredients into the high-speed blender and blend until nice and smooth. Serve and enjoy.

HEALTHY PLEASURE SMOOTHIES

A Quick Note: Living "healthy" has never tasted and felt so good! Drink to your health with these immune boosting and comforting smoothies.

It is always a great idea to drink a variety of smoothies to gain the very best health advantage from your drink. This section of smoothies is not just a list of healthy choices; they are packed with the power of protein in the purest form possible for your diet. Artificial sweeteners are intentionally avoided to ensure the healthiest choices for you. Moreover, this is the way we should all strive to drink all our smoothies — clean, natural and delightfully healthy.

Soothing Watermelon Smoothie

Preparation Time: *15 Minutes*
Calories: *149 calories*
Serving: *2*

Ingredients:
4 cups Watermelon - seedless chunks
1 cup fat-free plain Greek Yogurt (use your favorite flavor)
1 medium Lime, juiced
2 Ice Cubes
1 teaspoon Vanilla Extract

Directions:
Place all your yogurt, lime juice, watermelon chunks and vanilla into your blender and process until smooth or for about a minute. Add the ice cubes in the blender last and blend for desired consistency. Pour in a glass and serve.

Go Slim Raspberry Smoothie

Preparation Time: *15 Minutes*
Calories: *175*
Serving: *1*

Ingredients:
1 cup cold unsweetened Almond Milk
2 tablespoons Protein Powder, recommended - Garden of Life
RAW Protein (optional)
½ cup fresh or frozen Raspberries
4 Ice Cubes

Directions:
Place all ingredients into your blender and process until smooth or for about a minute. Pour in a glass and serve.

Grapefruit Energy Smoothie

Preparation Time: *15 Minutes*
Calories: 135 per serving
Serving: 2

Ingredients:
2 cups Strawberries, fresh or frozen
1 Sweet Apple, cored and chopped
1 inch Fresh Ginger, peeled and chopped
2 tablespoons Protein Powder, recommended - Garden of Life
RAW Protein (optional)
1 cup Water

Directions:
Combine all ingredients in a blender and process until smooth.
Serve and enjoy.

Strawberry Protein Smoothie

Preparation Time: *15 Minutes*
Calories: 345
Servings: 1

Ingredients:
2 tablespoons Protein Powder, recommended - Garden of Life
RAW Protein (optional)
1 cup Unsweetened Almond Milk
½ ripe Banana, sliced
3 Strawberries (hulled)
2 cups of ice

Directions:
Place all ingredients (except ice) into your blender and process until silky smooth. Add ice and blend for 1 minute or until smooth. Pour in a glass and serve.

Avocado Pear Smoothie

Preparation Time: *15 Minutes*
Calories: *370*
Serving: *1*

Ingredients:
½ medium sized ripe Avocado
1 cup Unsweetened Pear Nectar (add more as needed to reduce thickness)
2 tablespoons Protein Powder, recommended - Garden of Life RAW Protein (optional)
½ teaspoon Vanilla Extract
1 cup Ice Cubes

Directions:
Puree ingredients in a blender until smooth. Serve and enjoy.

Simple Strawberry Pleasure Smoothie

Preparation Time: *15 Minutes*
Calories: *304*
Servings: *1*

Ingredients:
5 large Strawberries
1 pitted Dates
½ cup of Unsweetened Almond Milk
1 cup of ice cubes

Directions:
Add ice cubes to blender first and blend until smooth.
Add remaining ingredients and blend on low speed until your smoothie is smooth enough. Pour in a glass and serve.

Sizzling Watermelon Smoothie

Preparation Time: *15 Minutes*
Calories: *147 per serving*
Servings: *2*

Ingredients
2 ½ cups Watermelon, flesh - seeds removed and diced
2/3 cups Galia Melon, flesh - diced
2 tablespoon fat-free plain Greek Yogurt
2 Pitted Dates (optional)
2 tablespoons Protein Powder, recommended - Garden of Life
RAW Protein (optional)
Crushed ice

Directions:
Place all your ingredients into the blender and process until smooth or for about a minute. Pour in a glass and serve.

Orange Protein Smoothie

Preparation Time: *15 Minutes*
Calories: *251 per serving*
Servings: *1*

Ingredients
1 cup freshly squeezed Orange Juice (chilled)
2 cup fat-free plain Greek Yogurt
2 tablespoons Protein Powder, recommended - Garden of Life RAW Protein (optional)
2 teaspoon Wheat Germ (optional)
2 pitted Dates

Directions:
Place all ingredients into your blender and process until smooth or for about a minute. Pour in a glass and serve.

Fresh Beet Smoothie

Preparation Time: *15 Minutes*
Calories: *160 per serving*
Servings: *2*

Ingredients
1 small Beetroot, peeled, chopped in parts, cooked
½ cup freshly squeezed Orange Juice
1 ½ cups fat-free plain Greek Yogurt
2 teaspoon Ginger Root, freshly grated
2 pitted Dates

Directions:
Place all ingredients into your blender and process until silky smooth. Pour in a glass and serve.

Healthy Low Carb Smoothie

Preparation Time: *15 Minutes*
Calories: *147 per serving*
Serving: *2*

Ingredients:
3 cups Spinach
½ cup Watermelon
1½ cups Cantaloupe
½ cup fresh Strawberries
½ cup fresh Raspberries
2 tablespoons Protein Powder, recommended - Garden of Life
RAW Protein (optional)
¾ cup ice cubes

Directions:
Place all your ingredients into the blender and process until smooth. Pour in a glass and serve.

Spiced Pumpkin Smoothie

Preparation Time: *15 Minutes*
Calories: *161 per serving*
Servings: *2*

Ingredients
½ cup Pumpkin Puree
1 cup Unsweetened Almond Milk
¼ cup fat-free plain Greek Yogurt
1 medium ripe Banana
5-6 ice cubes
¼ teaspoon Pumpkin Pie Spice (or a dash of some cinnamon, nutmeg and allspice)
2 pitted Dates

Directions:
Place all your ingredients into the blender and process until smooth or for about a minute. Pour in a glass and serve.

Fruity Avocado Smoothie

Preparation Time: 15 Minutes
Calories: 225
Serving: 2

Ingredients:
½ medium whole Avocado, pitted and peeled
2 medium ripe Bananas, sliced
½ cup Orange Juice
¼ cup fat-free plain Greek Yogurt
1 tablespoon Ginger, grated
¼ cup of Lime Juice (optional)
2 pitted Dates (optional)

Directions:
Place avocado, bananas, orange juice and yogurt into your blender and process until smooth. Add ginger and lime juice and blend until well combined and creamy. Pour in your glass and enjoy.

Cantaloupe Protein Smoothie

Preparation Time: 15 Minutes
Calories: *348*
Serving: 1

Ingredients:
1 medium ripe Banana, half frozen and cut in chunks
1 cup diced ripe Cantaloupe
½ cup fat-free plain Greek Yogurt (use your favorite flavor if preferred)
2 tablespoons Protein Powder, recommended - Garden of Life RAW Protein (optional)
¼ cup freshly squeezed Orange Juice
2 Pitted Dates

Directions:
Place all your ingredients into the blender and process until smooth. Pour in your glass and enjoy.

Pump-up Energy Smoothie

Preparation Time: *15 Minutes*
Calories: *266 per serving*
Serving: *2*

Ingredients:
2 tablespoons Protein Powder, recommended - Garden of Life RAW Protein (optional)
1 ripe Banana, sliced
½ cup Mango, peeled and diced
2 cups Spinach chopped
2 medium Carrots, peeled and sliced
1 medium Sweet Apple, cored, seeded, and quartered
2 pitted Dates
1 cup Water

Directions:
Place all your ingredients into the blender and process until smooth. Add more water for desired consistency where necessary. Pour in a glass and serve.

Plum-Plum Smoothie

Preparation Time: 15 Minutes
Calories: 175
Servings: 1

Ingredients
3 Plums (red or purple), halved & pitted
½ cup fat-free plain Greek Yogurt
½ cup Unsweetened Almond Milk

Directions:
Place all your ingredients into the blender and process until smooth or for about a minute. Pour in your glass and enjoy.

Peaches 'n' Avocado Cream Smoothie

Preparation Time: *15 Minutes*
Calories: *126 per serving*
Serving: *2*

Ingredients:
½ medium Avocado, pitted and peeled
1 Peach, pitted
½ cup of Unsweetened Almond Milk
2 Pitted Dates (optional)
4 Basil Leaves

Directions:
Place all your ingredients into the blender and process until smooth and creamy. Pour in a glass and serve.

Deluxe Apple Smoothie

Preparation Time*: 15 Minutes*
Calories: *110 per serving*
Servings: *2*

Ingredients
1 Apple - peeled, cored and chopped
1 cup Unsweetened Almond Milk
1 cup Apple Juice
¼ teaspoon freshly grated Nutmeg

Directions:
Place all your ingredients into the blender and process until smooth or for about a minute. Pour in a glass and enjoy.

Apricot Glory Smoothie

Preparation Time: *15 Minutes*
Calories: *191*
Servings: *1*

Ingredients:
2 Apricots, halved and pitted
¾ cup organic Apple Juice
¾ cup fat-free plain Greek Yogurt
1 Pitted Date

Directions:
Place all your ingredients into the blender and process until smooth or for about a minute. Pour in a glass and serve.

Low Fat Cantaloupe Smoothie

Preparation Time: *15 Minutes*
Calories: *127 per serving*
Serving: *2*

Ingredients:
½ ripe Cantaloupe, peeled, seeds removed and cut into chunks
1 cup unsweetened Almond Milk
1 cup fat-free plain or vanilla Greek Yogurt
¾ cup Crushed Ice
2 pitted Dates (optional)

Directions:
Place all your ingredients into the blender and process until smooth. Pour in a glass and serve.

Nectarine-powered Vanilla Smoothie

Preparation Time: *15 Minutes*
Calories: *275 per serving*
Serving: *2*

Ingredients:
3 Nectarines (Peach can be used as substitute), peeled and seeds removed
2 ripe Bananas, sliced
1 cup fat-free vanilla Greek Yogurt
Crushed ice
2 Pitted Dates (optional)

Directions:
Place the nectarines, bananas, yogurt and dates into your blender and process until smooth. Next, quarter fill the glasses with crushed ice, and top with the smoothie mixture, and enjoy.

Almond 'n' Celery Vanilla Smoothie

Preparation Time: *15 Minutes*
Calories: *311*
Serving: *1*

Ingredients:
4 Celery Stalks
1 medium Apple, diced
1 tablespoon Almond Butter (use homemade or without additives)
1 cup fat-free vanilla Greek Yogurt
¾ cup Ice Cubes
1 teaspoon Vanilla Extract

Directions:
Place all your ingredients into the blender and process until smooth. Pour in a glass and serve.

Fruity Broccoli Smoothie

Preparation Time: *15 Minutes*
Calories: *153 per serving*
Serving: *2*

Ingredients:
1 cup Fat-Free Plain Greek Yogurt
¼ cup Organic/Freshly Squeezed Orange Juice
¼ cup Unsweetened Almond Milk
¼ cup Frozen Broccoli Florets
¾ cup Frozen Organic Strawberries
¾ cup Frozen Organic Peaches
2 pitted Dates

Directions:
Blend all ingredients in a blender until smooth. Serve and enjoy.

Spiced Carrot Mango Smoothie

Preparation Time: *15 Minutes*
Calories: *187 per serving*
Serving: *2*

Ingredients:
2 cups Mangoes, diced (or frozen mango chunks)
½ cup Carrot Juice
½ cup Apple Juice
½ cup fat free plain Greek Yogurt
¼ teaspoon Grated Nutmeg
½ cup Ice Cubes (omit if using frozen mango chunks)
¼ teaspoon Vanilla Extract

Directions:
Puree all your ingredients in a blender until smooth. Serve and be comforted by the taste.

Tropical Rhythm Smoothie

Preparation Time: *15 Minutes*
Calories: *168*
Serving: *1*

Ingredients:
½ ripe Mango, peeled and chopped
1 Passion Fruit, pulp scooped out for use
½ Pineapple, peeled and cut into chunks
8-10 fresh lychees, peeled and seeds removed
Juice of 1 Lime
4 Ice Cubes

Directions:
Place all your ingredients into the blender and process until smooth. Pour in your glass and serve.

Sizzling Cantaloupe Smoothie

Preparation Time: *15 Minutes*
Calories: *260*
Serving: *1*

Ingredients:
½ Cantaloupe (peeled, seeded and sliced)
½ cup Apple Juice
¼ cup pitted Cherries
¼ cup Raspberries
3 Ice Cubes

Directions:
Place all your ingredients into the blender and process until smooth. Pour in your glass and serve.

Fiber Rich Peach Smoothie

Preparation Time: *15 Minutes*
Calories: *145*
Serving: *1*

Ingredients:
1 cup frozen Peaches, chopped
1 cup Unsweetened Almond Milk
1 tablespoon ground Flaxseed

Directions:
Combine all ingredients in a blender and process until smooth.
Serve and enjoy.

Carrot Deal Smoothie

Preparation Time: *15 Minutes*
Calories: *219*
Serving: *1*

Ingredients:
2 Baby Carrots, chopped
1 cup fresh Carrot Juice
1 cup fat free vanilla Greek Yogurt
¼ of a fresh Lime, peeled
4 Ice Cubes

Directions:
Combine all ingredients in a blender and process until smooth.
Serve and enjoy.

Pomegranate Detox Smoothie

Preparation Time: *15 Minutes*
Calories: 187 per serving
Servings: 2

Ingredients:
2 cups Mixed Frozen Berries (use your favorite berries)
1 cup Unsweetened Pomegranate Juice
2 tablespoons Protein Powder, recommended - Garden of Life
RAW Protein (optional)
1 cup Water

Directions:
Combine all ingredients in a blender and mix until smooth.
Serve and enjoy.

Refreshing Cantaloupe Smoothie

Preparation Time*: 15 Minutes*
Calories*: 102 per serving*
Serving*: 2*

Ingredients:
1 cup Cantaloupe
1 ripe Banana, frozen
½ cup of Coconut Water
½ cup of Ice Cubes

Directions:
Puree ingredients in a blender until smooth. Serve and enjoy.

Work-Out Smoothie

Preparation Time: *15 Minutes*
Calories: *134 per serving*
Serving: *2*

Ingredients:
¾ cup Coconut Water (or Water)
¾ cup Red Grapes
1 ripe Banana
1 cup of Kale
1 small Cucumber
½ cup of ice (optional)

Directions:
Place all the ingredients into your high-speed blender and blend until nice and smooth. Serve and enjoy.

Low-Calorie Peach Smoothie

Preparation Time*: 15 Minutes*
Calories*: 104 per serving*
Serving*: 2*

Ingredients:
1 cup Unsweetened Almond Milk
2 cups Peach Slices (peeled, or unpeeled)
½ teaspoon Ground Ginger
Handful of Ice Cubes
1 Pitted Date

Directions:
Place all the ingredients into your high-speed blender and blend until nice and smooth. Serve and enjoy.

Beet It Smoothie

Preparation Time*: 15 Minutes*
Calories*: 115 per serving*
Serving*: 2*

Ingredients:
4 Beetroots (Beets), peeled and cooked
2 cups Unsweetened Coconut Water (or Water)
2 cups Strawberries, frozen
1 Lime, juiced

Directions:
Place all your ingredients into a high-speed blender and blend
until nice and smooth. Serve and enjoy.

Immunogizer Smoothie

Preparation Time: *15 Minutes*
Calories: *362*
Serving: *1*

Ingredients:
1 cup ripe Mango, cubed
½ cup Unsweetened Almond Milk
1 tablespoon ground Almonds
1 cup Cantaloupe, chopped
½ cup fresh Pineapple, cubed
1 ripe Banana
Ice Cubes

Directions:
Place all your ingredients into the high-speed blender and blend until nice and smooth. Serve and enjoy.

HEALTHY DESSERT SMOOTHIES

A Quick Note: Dessert Smoothies? Oh, yes! This *Slim-It-Down* collection of healthy dessert smoothies are intended for those with a sweet tooth and are perfect for beating those sugar cravings. Try these easy smoothie recipes when you're ready for your next dessert or your next delicious smoothie.

Watermelon Ginger Smoothie

Preparation Time: *15 Minutes*
Calories: *101 per serving*
Serving: *2*

Ingredients:
2 cups seeded Watermelon Chunks
½ teaspoons Ground Ginger
1/8 teaspoons Almond Extract
1 cup Ice Cubes
½ cups fat-free plain Greek Yogurt
2 Pitted Dates (optional)

Directions:
Place all your ingredients into the blender and process until smooth. Serve and enjoy.

Chocolate Orange Smoothie

Preparation Time: *15 Minutes*
Calories: *196 per serving*
Serving: *2*

Ingredients:
¾ cup Espresso or strong Coffee, cold
2½ cup Unsweetened Almond Milk
1 cup fat-free vanilla Greek Yogurt
½ cup freshly squeezed Orange Juice
3 teaspoons unsweetened Cocoa Powder
2 pitted Dates
Ice Cubes, to serve

Directions:
Place all your ingredients into your blender and process until smooth. Pour in a glass and enjoy.

Chocolate Dream Smoothie

Preparation Time: *15 Minutes*
Calories: 203
Serving: 1

Ingredients:
¾ cup fat-free chocolate Greek Yogurt
¼ cup Unsweetened Almond Milk
1 medium ripe Banana, sliced
2-3 large ice cubes

Directions:
Place all your ingredients into the blender and process until smooth or for about a minute. Pour in a glass and drink to the healthy taste.

I Can't Believe It's Healthy Smoothie

Preparation Time*: 15 Minutes*
Calories: 159
Serving: 1

Ingredients:
½ cup of fat-free plain Greek Yogurt (frozen)
1½ tablespoons Espresso
2 teaspoons of Cocoa Powder
½ medium ripe Banana
4 small Ice Cubes

Directions:
Place all ingredients according to listed order in your blender and process at a high speed until smooth.

Carrot Fantasy Smoothie

Preparation Time: *15 Minutes*
Calories: 206 per serving
Serving: 2

Ingredients:
3 medium Carrots, peeled and chopped
1 cup canned Pumpkin
1½ cups fat-free vanilla Greek Yogurt (frozen)
1 cup freshly squeezed Orange Juice

Directions:
Place all ingredients into your blender and process until smooth. Pour in a glass and serve.

Avocado Mango Berry Mix Smoothie

Preparation Time*: 15 Minutes*
Calories*: 177 per serving*
Serving*: 2*

Ingredients:
½ cup unsweetened Coconut Water (or Water)
½ cup fresh Raspberries
½ cup fresh Blackberries
½ cup fresh Strawberries
½ cup fresh Blueberries
½ Mango
½ Avocado
½ cup crushed Ice

Directions:
Place all the ingredients into your high-speed blender and blend until nice and smooth. Serve and enjoy.

Berry Freeze Smoothie

Preparation Time: *15 Minutes*
Calories: *102 per serving*
Servings: *2*

Ingredients
1 cup frozen Blueberries
1 cup frozen Strawberries
½ cup Pineapple Juice
½ cup Orange Juice
1 cup fat-free plain Greek Yogurt
2 Pitted Dates
5 Ice Cubes

Directions:
Place the blueberries, strawberries, juices, yogurt, dates into your blender. Process until it is smooth. Add 6 ice cubes into your blender and process until smooth or for about an extra minute. Pour in a glass and serve.

Dates Delight Smoothie

Preparation Time: *15 Minutes*
Calories: *265 per serving*
Servings: *2*

Ingredients:
1 cup Unsweetened Almond Milk
1 cup fat-free plain Greek Yogurt
10 pitted Dates, pitted and coarsely chopped
¼ cup unsalted Almonds
4 ice cubes (optional based on your preference)

Directions:
Place all your ingredients in a blender and process until smooth or for about 2 minutes. Pour into glasses and serve.

Comforting Raspberry Smoothie

Preparation Time: *15 Minutes*
Calories: *176 per serving*
Serving: *2*

Ingredients:
1½ cups Fresh Raspberries
1 cup medium Frozen Ripe Mango, cubed
1 cup Fat-Free Plain Greek Yogurt
¼ teaspoon Vanilla Extract
2 Pitted Dates
¼ cup Water
3 Ice Cubes

Directions:
In a blender, blend all ingredients well until smooth. Serve.

Blueberry Almond Smoothie

Preparation Time: *15 Minutes*
Calories: *211*
Serving: *1*

Ingredients:
1 cup Coconut Water
1 cup Blueberries
1 tablespoon Almond Powder/Flour
½ teaspoon Almond Extract
½ ripe Banana, sliced
2 pitted Dates (optional)

Directions:
Place all your ingredients into the blender and process until smooth. Pour in a glass and enjoy the taste.

Really Fruity Vanilla Smoothie

Preparation Time: *15 Minutes*
Calories: *142 per serving*
Serving: *2*

Ingredients:
½ cup Unsweetened Almond Milk
½ cup organic Apple Juice
1 cup Strawberries
½ cup Peaches, cut into chunks
½ ripe Banana, cut into 1-inch pieces
2 pitted Dates (optional)
1 teaspoon Vanilla Extract
1 cup Ice Cubes

Directions:
Place all ingredients except ice into your blender and process at until smooth. Add ice cubes and continue to process until smooth. Pour in a glass and enjoy the taste.

Berry Peach Smoothie

Preparation Time: *15 Minutes*
Calories: *175*
Servings: *1*

Ingredients
1 cup Raspberries
1 medium Peach, pitted & chopped
¼ cup Unsweetened Almond Milk
½ cup fat-free plain Greek Yogurt

Directions:
Place all your ingredients into the blender and process until smooth or for about a minute. Pour in a glass and enjoy the taste.

Easy Pina Colada Smoothie

Preparation Time: *15 Minutes*
Calories: *241 per serving*
Serving: *2*

Ingredients:
½ cup Coconut Milk
½ cup Water
1 medium ripe Banana, cut into chunks
1 Orange, peeled and seeds removed
1 cup Pineapple chunks, frozen
¾ cup Mango chunks, frozen

Directions:
Add milk and water into the blender, followed by banana, orange, pineapple, mango.
Blend until smooth.

Rich Anti-Oxidant Smoothie

Preparation Time*: 15 Minutes*
Calories*: 101 per serving*
Serving*: 2*

Ingredients:
½ cup Frozen Blueberries
½ cup Pomegranate Juice
½ cup Raspberries
½ medium Orange, peeled
1 cup Crushed Ice

Directions:
Combine your ingredients in the blender and mix until smooth enough. Add more water if needed.

Super Anti-Aging Smoothie

Preparation Time: *15 Minutes*
Calories: *279 per serving*
Serving: *2*

Ingredients:
½ cup Goji Berries (soaked overnight to soften)
2 cups Water
2 medium Oranges, peeled
1 cup Spinach

Directions:
Combine your ingredients in your blender and mix until smooth enough. Serve and enjoy.

Fennel Goodness Smoothie

Preparation Time: *15 Minutes*
Calories: *182*
Serving: *1*

Ingredients:
1 medium Grapefruit, peeled
1 bulb of Fennel
2 large Carrots
1 slice of fresh Ginger (about a centimeter)
2 Pears, cored and chopped

Directions:
Combine your ingredients in the blender and mix until smooth.
Add a little water if needed. Serve and enjoy.

Age Defying Smoothie

Preparation Time: *15 Minutes*
Calories: *110 per serving*
Serving: *2*

Ingredients:
½ cup fat-free plain Greek Yogurt
¼ cup Orange Juice
2 cups fresh Baby Spinach
1 cup Kiwi, sliced
1 banana, cut up
¼ cup fresh Pineapple, cut into chunks
2 tablespoon Chia Seeds

Directions:
Combine your ingredients in the blender and blend until smooth enough. Add more water if needed. Serve and enjoy.

SLIM-IT-DOWN DIET TIPS FOR A NEW LIFESTYLE

Yes, *Slim-It-Diet Smoothies* are ideally great for your healthy lifestyle journey, but it won't forgive all your "diet sins". Here are some *Bonus Diet Tips* that are particularly helpful on the *6-Day Energy Giver* (days that you are not on the *Smoothie Fasting Day*) or to help you even further in achieving optimal health.

Diet Tip #1 – Establish Realistic Weight Loss Goals

As a foundation of reassurance and motivation, it is vital to establish weight loss goals at the time you commit to losing weight. Whether you want to lose 2 pounds or 50 pounds, setting realistic weight loss goals is the key for succeeding with the Slim-It-Down diet. One of the most important steps is to set realistic and achievable weight loss goals that are easy to attain. You must remember that the weight did not come on overnight and it surely will not come off overnight—despite what you have been told. Avoid setting weight loss goals that are unhealthy or unachievable. Many people find it helpful to set both short term and long term goals in their weight loss endeavors.

Medical experts have come to an agreement that it is safe to lose up to three pounds per week without causing any negative side effects. Studies have shown that individuals who lose more than this week will regain the weight after a time and may also experience low energy levels. It is best to consult your doctor in order to determine what amount of weight is safe for you to lose.

Here is a worthy example: a 400 pound person can safely lose 4 pounds per week, while a 200 pound person should only lose 2 pound per week.

Diet Tip #2 – Adjust your Diet on a Step by Step Basis

A gradual and slow step-by-step change from the ordinary mixed diet to a healthier food diet is best to avoid shocking the body. Changing your diet requires gentleness and patience. If you try too hard and make a radical diet change like eating all fruits for weeks on end you can quite easily become out of balance with weight loss, a wrinkled face, excess elimination, tooth problems, weakness and even depression.

If a normal person eating a normal diet begins eating just fruits they may become sick very quickly because the fruit stirs up the stored toxic material in the body and brings it to the surface to be eliminated via the skin and lungs primarily.

Go slowly and go gradually. For the meat eaters who want to give up meat, potatoes and cooked vegetables, alternatives such as avocados, natural raw cheese and natural raw home-made yogurt are great substitutes.

Also, each week you may consider exchanging one food habit for a healthier habit. Take it week by week. For instance, this week change the amount of sugar in your tea to half the usual amount. Next week cut down to a quarter and then cut it out completely the following week.

Diet Tip #3 – Pay Attention to Your Diet

For someone who is dieting to lose weight, there are several ways to monitor your diet. Monitoring your weight is important because dieting doesn't end when you lose all the weight you want to lose. Your diet is a big part of keeping you slim, and needs to be healthy, so make lifestyle changes rather than short-term ones.

You will need to make necessary adjustments like, replacing high-fat foods with those that are low in fat such as fruit, vegetables, unrefined carbohydrates and lower-fat dairy products, and by being more physically active.

It's also important to watch the size of your meal servings. Bear in mind that this can be challenging, because with time you can lose touch with what's a sensible amount of food. How to watch your diet:

- Try meat, fish, eggs and other protein-rich foods, such as lentils and beans which provide essential nutrients for growth and tissue repair. Additional nutrients can also be found in these protein foods, such as zinc, B vitamins, selenium and iron.

- For starchy foods you should ensure that it makes up about a third of your total daily energy intake. Choose unrefined types of starches that are good sources of fiber. High fiber foods will also help you to overcome hunger pangs and help to improve appetite control.

- For milk and dairy foods choose low-fat or reduced-fat versions to reduce the amount of calories in your diet. Daily recommended calories are 1900-2100 for women and 2400-2700 for men, respectively.

- You should reduce your intake of foods containing fat and/or unhealthy sugars much as possible. Eating healthily means including foods that are packed with nutrients rather than packed with energy.

- Watch your salt intake. A lot of salt comes from food that has been processed by some means; hence you should make low-salt choices and always read labels to check sodium content. On average, we eat over 50 per cent more salt than the recommended level and more than twice the amount we actually need.

Diet Tip #4 – Read Your Labels

According to a newly reported study, taking an extra minute to read over a nutritional label could help a person lose nearly 10 pounds. Furthermore, a U.S. National Health Interview Survey revealed that 74 percent of women read food labels as opposed to 58 percent of men.

Reading nutritional labels is becoming an important tool used my many weight and health watchers. It is a good practice to read labels before your purchases, and avoid packages with ingredients such as artificial flavorings, color, preservatives, high fructose corn syrup and trans-fats.

When it comes to food labels, here's what you should pay most attention to:

- Watch calories per serving: Food manufacturers use very subtle deception to make you think that their products have lower food is lower in calories at a quick glance.

- Avoid for cholesterol, trans-fat and saturated fat. Bad fats can increase your risk of heart disease by up to 30 per cent.

- Avoid high fructose corn syrup, processed sugars and corn sugar. These sugars are significant contributors in decreasing metabolism and increasing weight gain.

Diet Tip #5 – Ignore the Pretty Pictures

Just because there's a picture of fruit on the package doesn't mean that the package contains fruits. We see this pretty often with packages labeled as "fruit yogurts" or "fruit drinks".

It's not a secret that the weight loss industry as a whole has traditionally used deceptive advertising practices for products which either do not work or do not deliver the level of results promised. Pretty pictures such as before and after photos are a big part of this deception.

For weight-loss companies, the availability of celebrities willing to parade their weight loss success is one of the best marketing tools. People have been responding to testimonials by popular personalities for a very long time as these are far more influential stories than stories from ordinary people.

Hence, as consumers we should all learn to ignore the glamorous celebrity weight loss picture fad!

Diet Tip #6 – Get a Great Start Every Morning

Regularly eating a healthy breakfast may help you lose excess weight and maintain your weight loss. Even if you're not having your usual *Slim-It-Down Diet Smoothie*, you should ensure that you have a healthy breakfast.

Eating breakfast may get you on track to make healthier choices throughout the day. Medical practitioners have come to agree that by eating breakfast, people usually eat a healthier diet overall and one that has reduced fat. By skipping breakfast, it is more likely that you will practice unhealthy eating habits for the entire day as well.

Diet Tip #7 – Reduce Stress Naturally

Stress is a known contributor to significant weight gain. Furthermore, prolonged stress may cause serious increase in the body's level of harmful stress hormones.

Tips to De-stress for weight loss and good health:

- You should stick to the *Slim-It-Down Diet Smoothies* regime.

- Ensure that you get adequate sleep at nights.

- Do something that you enjoy and have fun. Some people rarely make time to do anything for self, especially anything enjoyable. Go and have some fun.

- Give yourself some pampering. Taking time for massages, a pedicure, and manicures, is a great idea.

- Get yourself a glass of water. Sound too easy? Drinking water as a means of reducing stress is a proven strategy.

Diet Tip #8 – Make a Coffee Switch To Green Tea

It is well known that the Japanese can give credit to green tea for their relatively good health and longevity.

For starters, green tea has zero calories, which makes it a smart beverage choice. It's much better than soft drinks or coffee with cream and sugar. Research has also linked an increased consumption of this green tea with a reduced risk of chronic health conditions such as heart disease and cancer.

Green tea consumption has also been associated with significant health benefits such as weight loss. People have reportedly shed a few pounds by simply swapping coffee for green tea. But more importantly, drinking green tea gives your metabolism a boost that causes your body to burn more fat. You can think of it as melting fat and converting it to energy. That's the real weight loss benefit that you'll get.

Diet Tip #9 – Have a Light Dinner

Having a light low calorie dinner is a great idea to add to any weight loss goal.

Think about it! What do most of us do after dinner? Yes, you're right... watch TV and then go to bed, or more or less of the two. Usually, we don't undertake any kind of activity that requires the body to spend the energy received at dinnertime. So all the body does is actually digest the food and store the FAT.

An ideal dinner would comprise of salads, soups and fruits. Home-made soups with veggies are most suitable, however low calorie canned soups can also be considered.

Diet Tip #10 – Make a Sweet Promise

There is countless research that has indicated that canned and bottled sugary beverages are a chief contributor to the obesity epidemic in the U.S.

In the end, sugary drinks will do nothing good towards our healthy lifestyle goals. Consequently, you should replacing sugary drinks with *Slim-It-Down Diet Smoothies* or water can improve your overall health and your weight.

So here's the deal: you should gradually reduce the amount of sugary drink in your diet until there is total elimination. Of course, you'll have those sweet cravings; however, there are lots of natural sugars in fruits which can satisfy those cravings.

Diet Tip #11 – Say Good-Bye to Unhealthy Fried Foods

By now, most of us know that fried foods are very rich in fats, even though they are also crispy and delicious. Today, many foods are fried to enhance flavor and appear more appealing.

Due to the health risks associated with frying foods which result from the high amounts of saturated and trans-fats, fried foods aren't among the healthiest.

While you are aiming to live a much healthier lifestyle, other healthier cooking alternatives are baking, grilling, toasting or steaming.

Diet Tip #12 – Stop When You're Full

Many of us struggle with overeating as we fail to resist larger portions of the food we love.

Without a doubt, overeating is the fastest way to ruin any diet and result in weight gain. If you really want to lose weight you'll need to stop eating when you're full. It is a much better idea to take home the remaining amount or leave it for the next day. Better yet, if you stick to your *Slim-It-Down Diet Smoothies* you will be better able to control regular hunger cravings.

So if you are having difficulty in this area, it's time to retrain your brain. Here are some quick tips:

- **Cut up your food:** Even though this may seem like a childish approach, cutting your food in smaller portions makes eating much more satisfying.

- **Eat your food slowly:** Many can attest to the fact that eating slowly can increase the odds of you feeling full sooner.

- **Chew your food properly**: Chewing your food into smaller pieces is a great way to curb overeating.

Usually, very little chewing may result in overindulging.

- **Become aware:** Being aware of how you feel before you consume your food will help you to determine what problems you may have when it comes to your connection with food.

- **Choose right:** Even if you're longing something unhealthy, getting proper knowledge and choosing healthy foods that fill you up like *Slim-It-Down Diet* smoothies, baked potatoes or eggs will leave you feeling much better for stretched than high-calorie junk will.

- **Take pleasure:** If you've continuously fallen victim to sugar and salty treats, it's time to redefine your feelings with healthy meals and *Slim-It-Down Diet Smoothies*.

- **Practice portion control:** When it comes to a healthy diet, we know that serving control is one of the keys to attainment. Giving your body the "I'm satisfied" indicator will help you to stop overeating.

Diet Tip #13 – Plan for a Sweet Snack

Craving for something sweet is perfectly natural and you shouldn't have to go without it. Planning for a sweet snack whenever you have your sweet craving can keep you satisfied and can even help along with your weight loss objectives. Here are a few ideas:

- Slim-It-Down Diet Smoothies

- Fresh Organic Cherries

- Fresh Organic Strawberries

- Orange Slices

- Fresh Organic Raspberries

- Raisins

- Fresh Organic Blueberries

- Fresh Organic Pomegranates

- Organic Greek Yogurt

- Apples

- Sweet Vegetables

- Goji Berries

- Dark Chocolate. Better than milk chocolate

- Dried Apricots

Diet Tip #14 – Develop Your Own Weight Loss Mantra

A mantra is what you make of it. It can be a quote or saying that you find to be inspirational, or it might even be a lyric to a favorite song. Creating your own weight loss mantra might be quite a motivational tool to help you reach your weight loss objective and to help you to be more focused. With a less pessimistic perspective about losing weight, there is a better chance of succeeding at it. This is why it is a good idea to make use of your weight loss mantra when you're feeling a bit less inspired? Here are some weight loss mantra ideas:

- If you were able to start it, you are surely able to finish it.

- I deserve to be healthy

- One moment at a time, I'm looking great and feeling better

- Yes I CAN

Diet Tip #15 – Avoid White Foods

White foods are a favorite with many people and are popular ingredients among packaged or processed food. Consequently, giving up white foods can be a tough task. White foods mainly include foods such as white pasta, salt, white sugar white bread, white flour, white rice and potatoes. Foods to choose instead of "White Foods" include:

- Colorful vegetables

- Fruit

- Lentils

- Chick Peas

- Whole Wheat Pasta

- Brown Rice

- Full Grain Breads

- Green Leafy Vegetables

- Yams

- Quinoa

- Black Beans

Diet Tip #16 – Choose Whole Grain Foods

Choosing to eat whole foods is basically about eating the way you were created to eat. Consequently, if your goal is to lose weight or improver overall health, it is essential that you eat natural and organic unprocessed foods.

Eating nutrition-rich foods such as fruits, vegetables and whole grains will be a sure way to support the lost pounds while powering up your body during exhaustive moments. Bear in mind that the USDA suggests that we consume at least three servings of whole grains every day for a part of a healthy diet. Here are some examples of whole grains:

- Whole wheat

- Whole oats/oatmeal

- Whole-grain barley

- Wild rice

- Buckwheat

- Bulgur (cracked wheat)

- Millet

- Quinoa

- Whole-grain corn

- Popcorn

- Brown rice

- Whole rye

Please note that you should look out for products that not whole-grain which are usually labeled like this: "cracked wheat "multi-grain," "stone-ground," "seven-grain," "bran" or "100% wheat,". As an alternative, you should look out for a decent amount of fiber as a good indicator of products that are whole grain. Another good indication is also to read the nutrition label on packages to see if the first ingredient listed is whole wheat or other wholegrain.

Diet Tip #17 – Go for a Little Neighborhood Adventure

Walking can be seen as an easy form of aerobic exercise. This makes walking around your neighborhood and sightseeing a great idea. Wherever you are, take a stroll around and expand your horizons while getting some exercise.

You may even consider adding some upbeat music to your walking adventure. Studies have shown that by adding upbeat music to your walking health routine it can help you to burn more calories.

By varying the speed of your walk you will also increase energy and tone your muscles much faster. Here is a quick walking guide:

- For the first few minutes of your walk, you should walk moderately.

- Whenever you want to catch your breath, slow down and walk normally.

- Continue to increase your speed as you walk briskly for at about 12 minutes.

- You may cool down your walking with a moderate 5 minute walk.

Diet Tip #18 – Add Crunchy Foods to Your Diet

It is proven that crunchy foods can truly suppress your hunger. While this is not the healthiest way to lose weight, it works like a charm. Crunchy food requires extra chewing and includes almonds, apples, carrots, sunflower seeds, broccoli, celery or chopped walnuts. By chewing more it is expected that you'll eat less.

Diet Tip #19 – Use Smaller Plates

You've probably heard that by using a smaller plate you may better control the portions that you eat, but, maybe you've not given it much thought.

Well, if you should think about it, substituting your 12-inch plate for a 10-inch one is not a bad idea. By doing this, you could end up eating up to 25% less and also reduce your calorie intake. In other words, changing the size of your plate could help you to lose up to 2 pounds in a single month.

This is how it works: if you should put a small amount of food on a big plate, your thoughts will tell you that you are consuming a small portion and you will spontaneously put more food on the plate. However, if you put that same amount of food on a small plate, your thoughts will tell you that you are eating a large portion and you'll stop putting more food on the plate.

Diet Tip #20 – Make a Tomato Ketchup Switch

The diet concern of ketchup is that it is made with a considerable amount of sugar, it stimulates sweet cravings and it also increases hunger. Consequently, if you are concerned about gaining weight, ketchup should not be on your food list.

Here are 2 ketchup alternatives for persons who want to lose weight:

- Salsa: This is simply a recipe combination of peppers and tomatoes and is really healthy when compared to ketchup. Homemade salsa would be your best option for benefiting from the host of essential vitamins and minerals that it can deliver to the body.

- Sun Dried Tomato Hummus: This works as a good alternative even though it is not technically a ketchup substitute. Sun dried tomato hummus works well on hamburgers and also on French fries plus staves off hunger pangs.

Diet Tip #21 – Outsmart Your Genes

Yes it is true! There are many factors that help to determine an individual's body size and shape, and there's absolutely no doubt that genetics plays a vital part in it. Maybe you may have noticed that you have a tendency to put on those pounds weight easily like your mother or probably you tend to gain weight in certain parts just like your daddy.

It is a certainty that quite a few studies have identified a gene known as the "fat gene" (known as the FTO gene). This gene is found to increase an individual's risk of becoming or being obese by an average of about 12 percent.

The reality is, anatomy should not define your destiny. If your parents or siblings are overweight, it doesn't mean that you have to be overweight too. You can outwit and retrain your genes with a healthy nutrition and regular exercise.

Diet Tip #22 – Build Muscles

You can change your body structure by making an effort to shedding fat and replacing it with muscle. How do you do this? To do this, you must commit to a healthy diet and exercise program that includes both cardio and strength training, on a fitting time schedule.

Even though replacing fat with muscle seems comparatively simple, when it comes to your food regime, it can become quite complex. While you'll need to reduce your calorie intake in order to lose some weight, you'll also need increase your calorie intake in order to grow your muscles. Consequently, in addition to your diet, you will also need to engage in moderate exercise in order to burn some calories and tone your muscles.

Remember to always check with your doctor before you embark on any exercise program.

Diet Tip #23 – Increase Your Energy

One of the simplest and quickest ways to increase your energy is by standing up. By standing up more blood will flow to the brain, thus increasing the oxygen level in the brain. You may also increase your energy level by simply brisk walking for a few minutes each day.

Other than dieting and exercise, here are three simple ways to increase your energy:

- *Drink Slim-It-Down Diet Smoothies on a daily or regular basis.*

- *Deep Breathing:* I knew that this came as I surprise to you. People who are into Yoga already know that deep breathing is one of the most significant ways of improving the energy level. This is an easy way to increase your energy and you can do this every morning, at noontime and in the evening simply by taking 10 very deep breaths. You may also begin breathing deeply by inhaling for about 7 seconds, holding your breath for about 28 seconds and exhaling for 14 about seconds.

- *Sleeping:* Maybe it seems obvious that getting enough sleep is important in order to be energetic for the next day. Be mindful that getting more than 8 hours of sleep may also stand to decrease your energy.

- *Have Positive Mental Thoughts:* Have you ever experienced how energy-consuming an emotional fight between you and someone else can be? Or have you realized how energy-draining certain thoughts can be? That's because our thoughts have an impact on our energy levels. Bear in mind that we have the power to choose what we think about. I believe that not being fully aware of our thoughts and feelings is one of the greatest hidden energy-drainer. Therefore we can benefit greatly if we learn to control what we think about.

Diet Tip #24 – Control Your Unhealthy Food Cravings

We all must admit that there are many irresistible foods out there. However, controlling your unhealthy food cravings is a great way to improve your weight loss objectives.

Here are four proven ways that you can take control of your food cravings, stay slim, and still feel full:

1. *Have Slim-It-Down Diet Smoothies*: Allow *Slim-It-Down Diet Smoothies* to be a regular part of your regular diet.

2. *Avoid your triggers:* Change one trigger at a time and you could really turn things around when it comes to craving for the wrong foods.

3. *Take control:* Always remember that you have the authority to make healthy food choices. Make the wisest choice.

4. *Stick to a schedule*: It is best to eat at a certain time in order to prevent thoughtless nibbling.

CONCLUSION

We'll never succeed at anything in life if we are negative. Being negative will drain the energy that we should use to progress successfully. With that being said, the only thing between you and your weight loss success is you. Be positive. Being overweight doesn't have to be a permanent condition, it can change. You can turn things around and obtain an ideal weight. If others have done it, so can you.

So many times, dieters are steaming with enthusiasm at the beginning of a weight loss program. But obviously, if we are serious about losing weight, it should definitely NOT be a "on-again off-again" approach. It's an approach that you have to stick with to really realize the benefits. Yes, you can be moderate with the *Slim-It-Down* approach and still lose weight, however, bear in mind that there are a host of other health benefits with this regime. With this information you will always have control over your weight and your energy level.

I'm thrilled to know that I have been able to assist you in losing weight and I'm also delighted to know that I've been able to ultimately contribute to improving your longevity. Even if you drift a bit from this diet and gain unwanted weight, years from now you will still be equipped with the recipes and information you've received in this book. Consequently, you will be able to turn your situation around whenever you wish. Always remember that staying healthy is your best option.

Ultimately, your own weight loss progress and overall healthier lifestyle can be as easy or as hard as you make it. By purchasing this book, you've shown that you have taken the responsibility for your own well-being. You most assuredly deserve it.

All the best!
Diane

More Books Written By Diane Sharpe

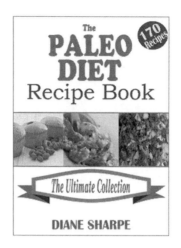

12521712R00109

Printed in Poland
by Amazon Fulfillment
Poland Sp. z o.o., Wrocław